Start to Finish
Second Series

Food

FROM Maple Tree TO Syrup

MELANIE MITCHELL

LERNER PUBLICATIONS COMPANY Minneapolis

Lerner Publications Company
A division of Lerner Publishing Group, Inc.
241 First Avenue North
Minneapolis, MN 55401 U.S.A.

Website address: www.lernerbooks.com

This book depicts the traditional process for collecting maple sap. This process is still used in many sugar bushes. However, modern sugar bushes also often use plastic tubing to collect sap.

Photo Acknowledgments
The images in this book are used with the permission of: © Danita Delimont/Gallo Images/Getty Images, p. 1; © Ryan McGinnis/Alamy, p. 3; Cornell Maple Program, p. 5; © Marilyn Angel Wynn/Nativestock/Getty Images, p. 7; © NaturePL/SuperStock, p. 9; © Joseph Mercier/Dreamstime.com, p. 11; © SuperStock, p. 13; © Joe Raedle/Getty Images, p. 15; © Major Pix/Alamy, p. 17; © Aaron Flaum/Alamy, p. 19; © Vicki Beaver/Alamy, p. 21; © Flirt/SuperStock, p. 23.

Front cover: © Gene Lee/Dreamstime.com.

Main body text set in Arta Std Book 20/26.
Typeface provided by International Typeface Corp.

Library of Congress Cataloging-in-Publication Data

Mitchell, Melanie (Melanie S.)
    From maple tree to syrup / by Melanie Mitchell.
        p. cm. — (Start to finish. Second series, Food)
    Includes index.
    ISBN 978-0-7613-9181-4 (lib. bdg. : alk. paper)
    1. Maple syrup—Juvenile literature. I. Title.
TP395.M57 2013
664'.132—dc23
                        2011036509

Manufactured in the United States of America
1 – DP – 7/15/12

TABLE OF Contents

Maple Syrup is sweet. How is it made?

Workers plant trees.

Maple syrup comes from sugar maple trees. Workers plant many sugar maple trees for making syrup. This group of trees is called a **sugar bush**.

The trees grow.

The sugar maple trees grow and make **sap**. Sap is a clear, sweet liquid. In early spring, the sap flows through the trees' trunks and branches. It is time to collect the sap.

Workers drill holes.

Workers drill small holes in sugar maple trees that are at least fifty years old. Only one hole is drilled in small trees. Two or three holes may be drilled in big trees.

Spouts are put in the holes.

Metal **spouts** are put into the holes in the trees. A spout is a tube that liquid can flow through.

Workers hang buckets.

Workers hang buckets on the spouts.
Sap flows out of the spouts. The
buckets collect the sap.

The buckets are emptied.

Workers empty the buckets full of sap into barrels. The buckets are put back on the spouts to collect more sap.

The barrels are taken away.

The barrels full of sap are taken to a **sugarhouse**. A sugarhouse is a place where maple syrup is made.

The sap is heated.

Workers pour the sap into long, shallow
pans. The pans of sap are heated. The
sap begins to boil. It becomes thick and
sticky. It has turned into maple syrup!

The maple syrup is poured.

The fresh maple syrup is poured into bottles and sent to stores. People buy the syrup and take it home.

Time to eat!

It's hard to believe this sweet treat came from a tree. Try some maple syrup on pancakes or ice cream. Enjoy!

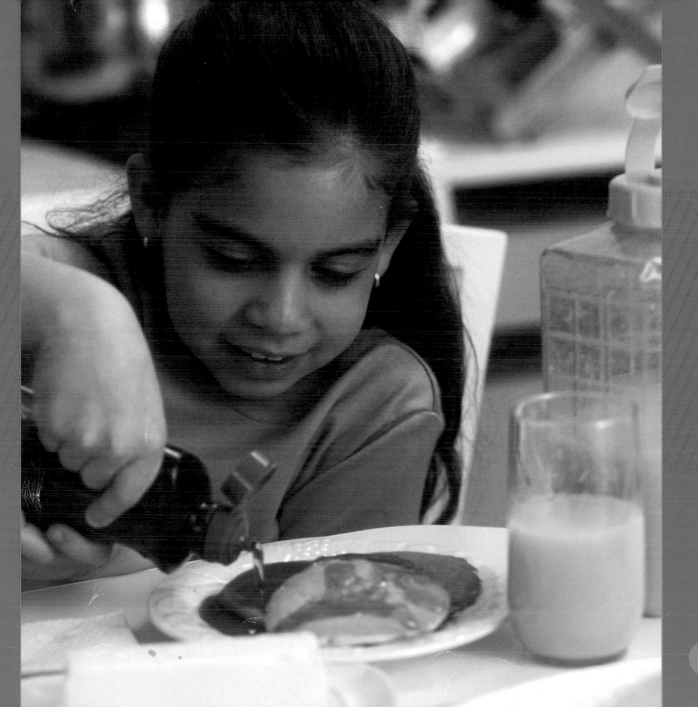

Glossary

sap (SAP): colorless liquid inside a tree that contains sugar

spouts (SPOWTZ): tubes that liquid flows through

sugar bush (SHU-gur BUSH): a group of sugar maple trees

sugarhouse (SHU-gur-hows): a building where maple syrup is made

Index